T0368699

MY EARLY LIFE

GUSTAVE FEISSEL

authorHOUSE®

AuthorHouse™
1663 Liberty Drive
Bloomington, IN 47403
www.authorhouse.com
Phone: 833-262-8899

Published by AuthorHouse 01/13/2025

ISBN: 979-8-8230-3797-6 (sc)
ISBN: 979-8-8230-3796-9 (e)

Library of Congress Control Number: 2024924471

Print information available on the last page.

MY EARLY LIFE

||||||||||||||||||||||

by Gustave Feissel

I decided to set out my early life because it represents my life in another world, a terrible world, a life full of anxiety and anguish. The period I will cover are my first thirteen years, the years before I emigrated from France to the United States in July 1950. I realized only in later years that my early life had a profound impact on my adult life. In retrospect, it was not a happy period. It was not a happy childhood. This was not because of my parents. My mother and father were loving and caring parents despite the difficult and dangerous environment in which they had to live. Their lives were shattered by the existing conditions first in Germany, and then in France. In short, the trauma of those years stemmed solely from our being Jewish.

My effort to piece together my first thirteen years was not easy: I did not keep a diary, my memory of my mother who died when I was twelve years old has largely faded, and I do not recall ever speaking to my father about his past or about our life together during this period. I have done the best I could through extensive research and discussions with persons familiar with the period I am covering. As a result, I have been able to put together a pretty good overview of my life during this period and of the events that marked those years. Although, as will become evident, questions remain unanswered. Writing about my early life has reawakened profound and sad emotions of long ago.

RESEARCH

||||||||||||||||||||||

In doing research about my early life I was fortunate to have at my disposal three excellent and very pertinent publications and to be in contact with the authors of these publications whose insights shed additional light on the subject covered in their books.

A university master's thesis written by Karin Sommer (1983) *"Die Juden von Altenstadt Zum Alltagsleben in einem Judendorf von ca. 1900-1942 (hrsg. vom Landkreis NeuUlm)"* (History of the Jews of Altenstadt, Everyday life in a Jewish village, 1900-1942). Ms. Sommer told me that she was prompted to write her study because, during her entire secondary school education in her native town of Altenstadt an der Iller, not a word was said about the Jews of Altenstadt, even though Jews had been such a major part of its

3

history. Her exhaustive study offered me a wealth of information about the history of the Jews in Altenstadt over almost three centuries that they had lived there (1650-1942). Hitler achieved his goal, there are no Jews left in Altenstadt. Ms. Sommer's master's thesis also revealed my father's history and gave me insights into his life and personality that I was not aware of. She brings out how courageous and outspoken my father was in reaction to the anti-semitism that prevailed in the 1930s.

I was also fortunate to have the benefit of two remarkable publications that brought to light details about life in the Dordogne, France, about the Jewish refugees who lived there during the war, and about the grave dangers faced by the refugees, especially Jews living there. The Dordogne is a department in the south western part of France, where my parents and I lived as refugees during the war (1941-1945).

One book is *"Les Juifs en Dordogne 1939-1944: De L'Accueil à la Persécution"* (2003) (The Jews in the Dordogne: from Welcome to Persecution 1939-1944) by Bernard Reviriego. It deals with the increasing persecution faced by the Jewish refugees in the Dordogne under the Vichy regime and German occupation. In his comprehensive study of this dark period in France, Mr. Reviriego notes that more than 1600 Jews of the 6300 Jews living in the Dordogne during World War Two were murdered by the Germans.

The second book "*La Cité Silencieuse: Strasbourg-Clairvivre 1939-1945*" (2019) by Christophe Woehrle (The Silent City: Strasbourg-Clairvivre 1939-1945) focusses on the transfer of the hospital of Strasbourg in Alsace, France, with 550 beds, and its doctors, staff, and patients to the village of Clairvivre in the Dordogne and its impact on Clairvivre during World War Two.

FAMILY BACKGROUND

||||||||||||||||||||||||||||

The lives of my parents and my life were profoundly shaped and shattered by events beginning with World War One, the inter-war period, and the advent of Hitler's Germany. My story must therefore begin long before I was born. It must start with the early years of my paternal grandparents and the birth of my father.

My paternal grandfather, Gustave Feissel, was born on November 17, 1877, in Hattstatt, a small village of a couple hundred inhabitants in southern Alsace, formerly France, but at the time was part of Germany, having been annexed by Germany following France's defeat in the Franco-Prussian war in 1871. Alsace reverted back to France at the end of World War One in 1918 and was then re-annexed by Germany in 1940 until 1945 when it reverted again back to France.

My paternal grandfather's family had lived in Hattstatt for several hundred years. Birth certificates of Feissels born in Hattstatt can be found dating to the early 1700s and probably goes prior to that time. My paternal ancestors were involved mainly in commerce. My paternal great grandfather and great grandmother, born in Hattstatt, were Felix Feissel (1839-1905) and Rosa Feissel (1842-1929). My paternal grandfather was a merchant. From information I was able to obtain, it would appear that my grandfather was a secular Jew. He belonged to the shooting club of Mulhouse, Alsace, and I have three silver shot glass trophies which he won in shooting competitions in Mulhouse, as well as two silver shot glass trophies which he won in shooting competitions in 1908 in Strasbourg, the largest city in Alsace (annex 1).

On February 17, 1903, my grandfather married Hedwig Einstein from Altenstadt an der Iller in Bavaria, Germany. Hedwig Einstein was born in Altenstadt on January 7, 1881. It would appear that she was also a secular Jew. She was a third cousin of Albert Einstein. After we came to the United States, my father thought about visiting

7

Albert Einstein in Princeton, but we never did. My paternal grandmother's family had lived in Altenstadt for almost two centuries. Her father was a jeweler. As their respective villages are some 220 miles apart, which at that time was a great distance, it is most likely that my grandfather met my grandmother through a match-maker, a frequent way for young Jews to meet persons from a wider area. They were married in Altenstadt on February 16, 1903, and then settled in the city of Mulhouse, Alsace, about 20 miles south of Hattstatt. On January 26, 1909, their only child, René Félix Feissel (my father), was born in Mulhouse.

Soon after the onset of World War One on July 28, 1914, my grandfather was drafted into the German army and died of a war related illness on September 4, 1914, at the age of 37. My grandfather's name is on three monuments: in Altenstadt in honor of the German soldiers from Altenstadt killed in World War One; in Illereichen-Altenstadt Jewish cemetery there is a plaque in honor of the three Jewish soldiers from the area, including my grandfather, fighting for Germany killed in World War One; and in

Hattstatt, France, his name is on the monument in honor of all persons born in Hattstatt who were killed fighting in World War One and World War Two. Following the death of her husband, my paternal grandmother and her son (my father) decided to leave Mulhouse and return to Altenstadt an der Iller, Germany, her native village.

Altenstadt is where my father lived for twenty five years from 1914 to 1939, where he married my mother in 1936, and where they lived until 1939, and where I was born in the hospital of the neighboring village of Illertissen on July 11, 1937. Altenstadt therefore represents an important part of the lives of my parents and the first two years of my life. It therefore deserves appropriate attention when writing about my early life.

Ms. Sommer explains in her study that Altenstadt an der Iller was a small village in Bavaria about 80 miles west of Munich. It had a sizable Jewish community dating back to 1650 when the first five Jewish families settled in Altenstadt. The Jewish community in Altenstadt grew to some 400 persons by 1835. It built its first synagogue, a wooden structure, in 1725. As the Jewish community of Altenstadt grew, a larger synagogue was constructed in stone in 1802 (annex 2). Its inauguration was attended by both Jews and non-Jews of Altenstadt. The synagogue was described by a contemporary art historian as one of the most monumental village synagogues that had been built, which reflected the importance of the Jewish community of Altenstadt. In 1803, a community center was built next to the synagogue which was used as a Jewish grammar school and also had a ritual bath for women. The Altenstadt Jewish community had a full-time rabbi as well as a full-time schoolmaster.

In 1834, the Altenstadt Jewish community comprised 56 families or some 400 persons, making up the majority of the population of Altenstadt at that time. The Jewish population remained the largest group in Altenstadt until the mid 1800s and was well integrated into the German society. For example, in the 1920s the Jewish community contributed to the construction of the church bell and the town administration helped to finance the building of the wall around the Jewish cemetery. At some point the Jewish population in Altenstadt began to decrease as younger persons moved to larger towns and cities and to the United States. By 1855, the Jewish population had fallen to some 250, and by 1933 was a mere 60 out of a total population of about 1000.

My paternal grandmother had a sister, Emma Marx, née Einstein, who also lived in Altenstadt and was married to a banker, Josef Marx. When Josef Marx died in 1903, the house in which the bank was located was transferred to Emma Marx who dissolved the bank. In 1922, my paternal grandmother married a local merchant, David Maier who died in 1926. They rented Emma Marx's house to open a clothing store on the main floor. My father, his mother, and his step-father lived on the upper floor. My grandmother's sister, Emma Marx, and her daughter Karolina also lived there. Later, the store was owned jointly by my grandmother and my father. After my father and mother were married they moved into an apartment above the store. Emma Marx died in Altenstadt on May 2, 1939.

Now let me introduce my mother's family.

My mother's parents, David Wild and Babette Wild, née Kettner, married in the small village of Dormitz, where David Wild's family had lived for generations. After their wedding, they moved to Cronheim, about 60 miles south where Babette Kettner was from. My mother was born in Cronheim on June 12, 1905, the youngest of six sisters. David Wild was a farmer and green grocer, and became the head of the Cronheim Jewish community. Fortunately, my mother's parents died before the advent of Nazi Germany and were spared the tragedy and horrors that was to follow.

My mother's family was devastated by the holocaust. Her sister Klara Fleischmann (née Wild), her husband Heinrich Fleischmann, and their daughter Alice; her sister Betty Weimersheimer (née Wild), her husband Moritz Israel Weimersheimer, and their daughter Peppi Betty; her sister Emmy Neuberger (née Wild), her husband Leo Neuberger, their daughter Alice, and their son Walter were all taken from their homes in Cronheim and murdered in extermination camps in Poland in April,1942. I am attaching a photo of one of my young cousins holding me when I was fourteen months old. Three and a half years later she will be murdered in an extermination camp (annex 3).

Fortunately, two of my mother's sisters, Gertrud Einstein and Frida Einstein and their husbands (two brothers, Arthur and Bruno Einstein) emigrated to the United States in 1938. Ernest, the son of Klara Fleischmann, and Sam and Fritz, the two sons of Betty Weimersheimer, had also emigrated to the United States before the war. All three served in the United States armed forces during World War Two. Needless to say, the tragedies that befell my mother's family weighed heavily on my mother and father during and after the war.

THE IMPENDING DISASTER

|||||||||||||||||||||||||

Following the defeat of Germany in 1918, there was a dramatic surge of anti-semitism in Germany even though Jews had actively supported Germany during World War One.

The commemoration in 1919 for the three Jews from Altenstadt who were killed in WWI (including my grandfather) was the last time that Jews and Christians attended a Jewish event together in Altenstadt. Anti-semitic vandalism in Altenstadt became more prevalent beginning in 1922 when stones were thrown at the synagogue breaking its windows and in 1928 when gravestones at the Jewish cemetery were desecrated.

After Hitler came to power through existing legal processes in 1933, the situation took a dramatic turn for the worse. At that time, Altenstadt had a population of some 1100 persons, including some 50 Jews.

On May 7, 1936, my father married Martha Wild from Cronheim. No doubt they met through a match-maker. For their honeymoon my parents went to Milano, Italy. I remember my mother's suitcase which had a sticker from the hotel where they stayed. I still have several dish towels with the initials MW (i.e., Martha Wild) which were among the objects that my mother brought to the marriage and which somehow survived all the dislocations to come.

About this time, in the mid-1930s, major Nazi demonstrations took place in Altenstadt on an ongoing basis and frequent demonstrations took place in front of the store of my grandmother and father which was located on the main street of Altenstadt across the street from the Gasthaus Rose which was a meeting place of the local Nazi party. I was surprised to learn from Ms. Sommer's study how outspoken and courageous my father was in reaction to the growing anti-semitism in Altenstadt. He did not hesitate to speak out, which in turn increased the attacks against my father and the store. For example, during the demonstrations of November 10, 1938, a large group of Germans went to our house, knocked down the door, ransacked the apartment, and attempted to take my father. Fortunately, as a French citizen, he was taken into protective custody by the police where he was kept safe overnight. One can well imagine the fear experienced by my parents, my grandmother, and me, a toddler, as well as by other Jews of Altenstadt, during these many Nazi demonstrations. On a number of occasions, my father had to ask the French consulate in Munich to intervene on his behalf.

As an aside, I was surprised to learn from Ms. Sommer's study that even though my father had never lived in France (He was born in Mulhouse when it was part of Germany and at the age of five moved to Altenstadt in Germany), my father considered himself French. In 1929, at the age of 20, my father went to France to do his military service and then returned to Altenstadt.

With the adoption of the Nuremberg Racial Laws of September 15, 1935, anti-semitism became rampant and the sphere of activity open to Jews became increasingly limited. By 1938 all Jewish lawyers, doctors, dentists, pharmacists, and veterinarians were banned from practicing their professions. Jewish musicians and artists were banned from orchestras and theaters. Jews were even forced to get rid of their pets.

By 1936, the relations between Jews and Christians became extremely difficult. Laws were enacted which required Christians to boycott Jewish stores. Jews of Altenstadt saw their economic and social activities shrink dramatically. The store of my grandmother and father was no exception. While some older inhabitants still shopped in Jewish stores, they would only do so after dark. Soon Jews lost any semblance of normal life. They were excluded not only professionally but were also excluded from all cultural and social activities, public transportation, and parks.

Nazi sympathizers permeated social organizations and schools. On November 9, 1938, the so-called Kristallnacht erupted all over Germany following the death of a German officer who had been shot days earlier by a Jewish teenager in

Paris. That same night, German stormtroopers and Hitler Jugend went on a rampage all over Germany damaging 1400 synagogues and totally destroying some 250, destroying some 7,000 Jewish owned businesses, killing some 300 Jews that night, and subsequently sending some 30,000 Jews to Dachau and Buchenwald, Germany's first extermination camps. To add insult to injury, Jews were required to pay one billion Reich marks in damages.

This was only the beginning. What followed during World War Two is beyond comprehension. Poland had the largest Jewish population in the world. At the end of the war, the Germans and their collaborators had murdered 90% of the 3 million Polish Jews. Similar percentages apply to other Central and Eastern European countries.

The people of Altenstadt had their own Kristallnacht one day later. The tavern across the street from the synagogue of Altenstadt was also a meeting place of Nazi groups, with the consequences one can imagine. On November 10,1938, the interior of the Jewish synagogue was ransacked. It ceased being a house of worship and was turned by the local authorities into a warehouse. The next day, the local newspaper headlined "One less eyesore". In the middle of this terror were my grandmother and my parents with me, their 18-month-old son.

As an aside, the synagogue building itself survived the war. In 1951, the government of Altenstadt approved demolishing the historic synagogue built in 1802 and replacing it with a residential and commercial building!! This took place in 1955. In 1984, some residents of Altenstadt wanted to install a memorial plaque in memory of the synagogue and of the Jewish community of Altenstadt. It was met with indifference. Finally, in 1998, the area where the synagogue had been located was redesigned as a memorial park. The square was renamed "Hermann Rose Platz" in memory of the last teacher of the Jewish community of Altenstadt. A plaque was installed which states in German: "The synagogue of the Jewish community of Altenstadt which was built in 1802 stood here. It was damaged during the persecution of our Jewish fellow citizens in November 1938 and was demolished in 1955.

Grass withers, flowers wither, but the word of God endures forever".

As the situation in Germany became increasingly worse for Jews, my parents decided to leave Altenstadt for Mulhouse, France, my father's native city. On March 27, 1939, five months before the start of World War Two, my parents and I emigrated from Altenstadt, Germany, to Mulhouse, France, using our French passports (annex 4).

The question that has been on my mind for many years and for which I will never have an answer is why my grandmother did not come with us when we emigrated to France. It should have been possible for my grandmother to emigrate to France with us since she had been married to someone who was born in a village which, like Mulhouse, was considered part of France, even during the period it had been annexed by Germany. The French government therefore considered my grandmother a French citizen by marriage. How this must have weighed on the mind of my father. Unfortunately, by the time this question occurred to me my father had passed. On further reflection, it is quite possible that my grandmother decided that at her age she did not want to leave her native village where she had lived almost her entire life and move to a foreign country. A deadly mistake.

After our departure, the situation for Jews in Germany and in Altenstadt became unbearable. Jews were required to sell their houses and properties for next to nothing and were required to move into a single overcrowded house for Jews. For most Jews living in Germany there was no escape. At the end of 1938, there were still 32 Jews living in Altenstadt. They were all deported to extermination camps and murdered.

The final act came on March 31, 1942. On that day, the six remaining Jews of Altenstadt, including my grandmother and her niece Karolina Marx, were notified to be at the train station the next morning. They did not know where they were going. It was the end. They where taken to the extermination camp at Theresienstadt where they were murdered. On that day, the mayor of Altenstadt announced that Altenstadt was now free of Jews. Thus, after almost 300 years, the

Jewish Community of Altenstadt came to an end. As I mentioned earlier, at the same time, three sisters of my mother and their families who lived in Cronheim were sent to extermination camps and murdered.

It is ironic, if that is the proper word, that my grandmother, who was married to a person who was killed fighting for Germany in World War One, would be murdered by the Germans in World War Two.

MY STORY

|||||||||||||||||||||||||

I will now transition to my early life in France starting with my life during World War Two (1939-1945), age two to eight.

Soon after our arrival in France in late March 1939, we settled in an apartment at 32 rue de Sausheim in Mulhouse. Within a few months after the start of the Second World War in the autumn of 1939, my father was drafted into the French army (annex 5). He should not have been drafted at all since he had suffered from rheumatic fever as a child. He did not recall that, and his condition was not discovered when he was drafted. Not understanding the complexities of the adult world, as a two year old, I only realized that my father was no longer at home.

With the approaching war, the government of France had decided that most of the population living closest to the German border would be evacuated from Alsace and settled in several departments in southwestern France, including the Dordogne. After the German army entered Alsace on June 18, 1940, it invited Alsatian refugees who had left Alsace to return to their homes in Alsace, except those it considered undesirable, i.e., Jews, francophiles, and foreigners. Most Alsatian refugees who had been evacuated prior to the war accepted Germany's offer to return to their homes in Alsace, but some 40,000 refused to return.

The German army entered Mulhouse on 18 June 1940. On July 13, 1940 the Germans adopted a decree expelling all Jews from Alsace. My mother and I were among 109 Jews expelled from Alsace-Lorraine on July 17, 1940. We lost all our belongings as we were expelled. My mother carried with her the few treasures and photographs I have from our prior life (annex 1).

Our first destination was the French city of Lyon in central eastern France. We and the other Jews expelled from Alsace-Lorraine were lodged for several weeks in the hallways of the Palais de la Foire, a large covered central market where we slept on the floor. I don't recall the details of how we obtained food, blankets, sanitary facilities, etc. We left Lyon at the end of August 1940, and at the beginning of September 1940, 79 of the 109 Jewish refugees who had been expelled, including my mother and me, were sent to an internment camp located in Chaudanne-Castellane in the Basses Alpes in southeastern France. Chaudanne-Castellane was one several such camps located in that area. The others were sent elsewhere in the Basses Alpes. The refugee camps were not welcoming facilities for Jews, some of the Jewish refugees were arrested and deported.

The situation for Jews in France grew dramatically worse after the establishment by the Vichy government of France early in 1941 of the Commissariat Générale aux Questions Juives (General Commission for Jewish Questions). One of the most notorious laws called for taking a detailed census of all Jews living in each department of Vichy France. The Prefect responsible for the Basses Alpes department, Marcel Ribière, applied these laws rigorously. This information was published and then given to the French police and to the Germans. This greatly facilitated the many roundups that followed throughout Vichy France. I am attaching a copy of part of the document issued by the authorities of the department of the Basses-Alpes listing the 109 Jews from Alsace and Lorraine living in the department of the Basses-Alpes at the end of 1940. You will find there the names of my mother and me (annex 7). With the benefit of hindsight, I can say that we were lucky that we left Chaudanne-Castellane in early June 1941, as soon thereafter began the serious crackdown against Jews in the Basses Alpes including the deportation of many to extermination camps.

In May 1940, my father, was wounded in battle, further aggravating his general health and the heart condition he would suffer from the rest of his life. He was hospitalized in the city of Dijon in eastern France. While he was in the hospital, he was taken prisoner by the German army on July 2, 1940, and initially incarcerated in the German prisoner of war camp in the city of Belfort, France. On October 7, 1940, along with other Jewish prisoners, he was transferred to Stalag 17A, a German prisoner of war camp in Kaisersteinbruch, Austria. Following the armistice agreement between Germany and France, my father was released by the Germans for health reasons and repatriated to Notre Dame de Lourdes in France where he received further hospital care. It was most fortunate for my father that during the early months of the war, the German army still adhered to international prisoner of war regulations regardless of religion.

During all that time my mother had to fend for the two of us under very difficult circumstances and being frequently on the move for almost two years. Since most Alsatian refugees and Alsatian administrators spoke Alsatian German the language situation was manageable. My father was demobilized on January 20, 1941, and rejoined my mother and me shortly thereafter in Chaudanne-Castellane, after having been separated from us for one and a half years. I was three and a half. Whether or not I recognized my father when he returned, I can not recall. We stayed in Chaudanne-Castellane until the beginning of June, 1941, when we were moved to Clairvivre in the Dordogne in southwestern

France. It is quite possible that we were sent to Clairvivre because my father was wounded in the war and had a heart condition and Clairvivre had a major hospital. We arrived in Clairvivre on June 3, 1941, and stayed there to the end of the war in June 1945. Thus Clairvivre represents a major part of my early life, from age four to eight.

The small town of Clairvivre was unique. It was nothing short of a futuristic oasis in a primitive wooded farming area. In the early 1930s, the French government had decided to build a cité sanitaire in Clairvivre with a large sanatorium to treat the many veterans of the First World War who had been gassed in combat, and to treat persons suffering from tuberculosis. This immense building of some eight stories and several blocks long, built in the Belle Epoque style, would have been remarkable anywhere but was even more so in the middle of nowhere in rural France. Prior to World War Two, the only inhabitants of Clairvivre were the patients staying at the sanatorium and the physicians and staff looking after them.

With the approaching war, the government of France had decided, in August 1939, to move the population and the government administrations, hospitals, and banks from the Bas Rhin of Alsace to various departments in the southwestern part of France. That included moving the large hospital of Strasbourg lock, stock, and barrel, including its patients and physicians, to Clairvivre in the Dordogne which became known as the Hôpital des Réfugiés de Clairvivre (Hospital for Refugees of Clairvivre), some 500 miles southwest of Strasbourg (Google "Clairvivre France" to see photographs of this amazing facility).

The sanatorium was a perfect ready-made site for the hospital. It was self-sufficient, with space for doctors, nurses, and the administration for a hospital that could handle 550 patients. It had all the supporting requirements such as kitchen, laundry, printshop, garage, repair shop, store, etc. In addition, Clairvivre had some 350 apartments in 177 two family houses which could absorb the incoming hospital doctors and staff that could not be accommodated in the hospital complex. It would also accommodate refugees from Alsace that were arriving from 1939-1941.

In July 1941, the hospital at Clairvivre was ordered to dismiss all Jewish doctors and staff. Mr. Marc Lucius, the director of the hospital, made extraordinary efforts to maintain the Jewish physicians, by omitting some names from the requested list and by hiding others. He also made every effort to avoid hospital personnel from being sent to compulsory labor service in Germany. The cemetery of Clairvivre with its 682 graves, including Jewish graves, is a testimony to the challenging days during World War Two.

My parents and I arrived in Clairvivre on 3 June 1941. In Clairvivre we were housed in one of the aforementioned houses with two apartments. We first lived in pavillon 141 bis and then in pavillon 120 bis (annex 5). As a veteran, a former prisoner of war, and an invalid, my father was unable to work. He received a modest pension from the government, which helped us survive.

I have no recollection of who lived in the other apartment of our house, nor do I recall what our apartment looked like. As an aside, it is safe to assume that my parents, given my young age, had never talked to me about the birds and bees.

At some time, I must have told my parents that I wanted a brother. Somehow I remember that they told me to put a piece of sugar on the window sill, and that a stork would come, take the sugar, and leave a brother. It did not work.

I do recall that we had a large garden in the back of the house. We planted many vegetables such as potatoes, string beans, carrots, cabbage, cucumbers, lettuce, and melons, giving us our main supply of fresh produces. We also grew tobacco with which my father made cigarettes. We dug a hole in the ground where we placed the vegetables to preserve them (obviously we had no refrigerator or ice). In front of the house we had a chestnut tree. Each year we would harvest the chestnuts and grind them to make cooking oil. I always looked forward with great anticipation to eating the residue of the ground chestnuts. That may not have been healthy but was so delicious. We had one white chicken which became my pet, and she provided us with a few eggs each week. At some point the chicken became ill and had to be put away. It made me very sad. Frequently, my father would walk to the farms in the nearby area to purchase items such as butter, milk, eggs, vegetables, and meat. I recall, I would sometimes go with my father, and I would sit on his knapsack when I was tired.

With the large influx of hospital staff and refugees in 1940-1941, a school was established in Clairvivre for the children of the incoming families. The coed elementary class I attended had an Alsatian lady teacher and some twenty refugee students of similar age (see annex 8 photo of my class). I seem to recall vaguely that at some period, I don't know why or for how long, I went to a parochial school in Clairvivre run by nuns from the local convent. Since I was Jewish, I did not have to attend the daily religion class and could therefore arrive one hour later.

It was not easy being a care-free kid over the span of years as a refugee, but I did manage. Some of my school friends and I would, of course, get together to play. I only recall one activity we played at. We would go to the local cemetery where we would make believe that we were an honor guard and with wooden toy rifles perform a twenty-onegun salute in honor of a fallen maquis (French resistance fighters). Since the Dordogne was a very active maquis area, we would have witnessed frequent ceremonies for fallen resistance fighters.

The department of the Dordogne and nearby departments were rural areas with rolling hills and many forests, making it very conducive for guerrilla warfare. It was therefore the part of France where the French maquis was most active. As a result, it was also an area where the German army and the French collaborators were frequently present.

We lived under constant fear that the Germans or the Milice (French collaborators) would come through Clairvivre while we were there. We were frequently alerted "through the grapevine" that the Germans might be coming through Clairvivre. We immediately had to get out of town and hide in the nearby forest until they were gone. If Jews or persons suspected to be sympathetic to the French underground were caught, they would be either shot on the spot or deported to extermination camps. I recall that on one occasion, when we had to hide in the forest, I was sick. My parents left me at the local convent until they returned.

In addition to our every day concerns of surviving the dangerous conditions under which we had to live, my parents were also deeply worried about what had happened to my father's mother, and to my mother's three sisters and family living in Germany. They feared the worst, but did not know. Their concerns were well founded. They were all murdered.

By chance, a relative with whom I have been in touch about our family genealogy, found a letter which my mother had hand written in German from Clairvivre to her sisters Gertrud and Frida Einstein in New York, dated September 29, 1942. He had discovered the letter, among the papers of his grandmother who was the sister of Arthur and Bruno Einstein, the husbands of my mother's sisters in New York. It is a touching letter revealing the fear and anxiety that permeated my parents' lives. This letter from my mother written in her own hand writing is one of the few tangible links I have with my mother. It is interesting to note that in her letter written in German my mother signed her name in the French spelling Marthe.

In her letter (annex 6), my mother writes how pleased she was to have received a letter from them after such a long silence (during the war, mail from/to the United States and France was by sea and very irregular to say the least). She writes that she is very pleased that they are well and adds how lucky they are not having to live "in constant fear and worries". She expresses her appreciation that her sisters are making arrangements to obtain the papers for our emigration to the United States but wonders when that might be possible. My mother expresses her apprehension that she has not heard from her sisters and family in Germany for quite a while and adds that she fears the worst (we know now that by the time my mother's letter arrived in New York, her three sisters and family in Germany had all been murdered). She notes that we had been on the move for two years and expresses the hope that we would be spared from having to move again. She mentions that I am a big five year old boy and that in July 1942, I was in the hospital for a couple of days to have my tonsils removed, and that in a few days I would return to nursery school. She mentions that the conditions under which we have to live has made my father easily agitated. She adds that my father has had frequent problems with his heart and that his doctor had advised him to avoid strenuous activities. In my mother's letter, I note that my parents called me "Gusti" (the Alsatian and western German diminutive for Gustave), a name which I had completely forgotten. My father also added a message in the letter. Unfortunately, my father's handwriting made it difficult to read his message.

Life as a Jew in France during the war became increasingly precarious. Some 330,000 Jews lived in France at the outset of the war. By 1944, some 77,000 Jews had been arrested and deported from France to extermination camps. On June 25, 1941, the Vichy government passed laws excluding Jews from professions (e.g., maximum of 2% of doctors could be Jewish), the armed forces and universities, and requested each municipality to provide a list of the Jewish population living in their municipality. Jews living in France who were not French citizens were treated even more severely. Major roundups were organized on the basis of lists of Jews provided by the local authorities. In September 1941, the survey revealed that there were 6300 Jews in the Dordogne of whom 3,800 were French Jews. Of these 1,600 were murdered during the war. In 1942, the Vichy government decided to require that identity cards of Jews must state in large letters "Jew". My father's and my mother's identity cards had "JUIF" (Jew) written in the upper right hand corner (annex 7). Obviously, if the wrong person asked for your identity card, that was the end. The situation became even worse, especially for Jews, when in November 1942 all of France was occupied by the German army.

In collecting information for this paper I discovered that my family was not listed among the inhabitants of Clairvivre - a commendable act by someone in the town of Salagnac administration (of which Clairvivre was a part) to protect us. That kindness may have saved our lives.

During the war, several hundred wounded French underground fighters were surreptitiously treated at the hospital in Clairvivre thanks to the involvement of the hospital director Mr. Marc Lucius and the head of surgery Professor René Fontaine and their medical staff.

The hospital was very active in caring for and hiding refugees, including numerous Jewish refugees. Some thirty Jewish babies were born at the hospital from 1942 to 1944, not identified as Jews. Frequently, Jewish refugees were admitted under false names and under the pretense of having a serious illness. I remember that on several occasions, for reasons that I do not recall, my father was admitted to the hospital to protect him from danger. At one time, I recall that a sign was placed on the door of his hospital room which stated "Warning! Contagious Disease".

As mentioned earlier, the Dordogne was one of the departments where the French underground (the maquis) was most active. The roundups carried out by the Vichy government focussed mainly on foreign Jews. However, the Germans did not make that distinction. There were frequent roundups by Germans from 1943 onward. A major roundup took place in the Dordogne in February, 1943, in reaction to the killing of two German officers. Two thousand Jews were rounded up by the Germans on the basis of lists provided by the French government. Jews were shipped to the transit camp in Drancy, near Paris, and from there to the extermination camps at Sobibor and Maïdanek and to almost certain death. A frequent practice by Germans was to block off a street at each intersection and then ask for the identity card of every person caught inside and arrest all Jews for deportation.

The situation became worse in 1944 with the arrival in the Dordogne of the notorious Brehmer SS division and Das Reich SS division. Their focus was on killing Jews, underground fighters, and their sympathizers. Numerous examples could be listed where German troops, often supported by French collaborators, went through villages in the Dordogne, killing and deporting, and burning houses.

I will set out just a few examples which all took place very near to where we lived. In the early morning of April 1, 1944, some 200 German soldiers entered Sainte-Orse, a small village about 10 miles south of Clairvivre, where quite a few Jewish refugees lived. They shot 8 Jews and arrested 30 Jews who were sent to Drancy and then to Auschwitz-Birkenau extermination camp. Some ten Jews were hidden in the woods and survived thanks to the courage of non-Jewish inhabitants, whose names are inscribed on the "List of the Righteous Among the Nations" at Yad Vashem in Jerusalem honoring Christians who protected Jews. On another occasion, on June 9, 1944, in reaction to the killing of a German officer, the infamous Das Reich SS division rounded up 99 men and hanged them from balconies in the town of Tulle, some 25 miles east from Clairvivre. A most atrocious event took place on 10 June 1944, in Oradour-sur-Glane, a village some 60 miles north of Clairvivre. The Das Reich SS division massacred the entire population of 643 inhabitants, including 247 children. During this period of heightened German activity in the Dordogne, Marc Lucius and the hospital staff were very active in hiding Jews and resistance fighters.

Germans did not come to Clairvivre very often, but we only know this with the benefit of hindsight. From my readings, I learned that the Germans were reluctant to come through Clairvivre, because they were concerned about catching tuberculosis from the patients at the sanatorium.

An event which touched us personally, that is stranger than fiction, is worth recalling. We knew a Jewish family, originally from Germany, who had emigrated to France in 1933. The family comprised the parents Willy and Paulette Baer and their two daughters Ellen and Trudy. They were refugees from Strasbourg who lived in the tiny village of Saint Pancrace some 35 miles west of Clairvivre. We got to know them, because on occasion they would come to Clairvivre for medical treatment at the hospital. On March 27, 1944, Trudy was lucky to be in Clairvivre for treatment. Unaware that the Germans were coming through Saint Pancrace, the Baers were arrested at home. Willy Baer and other men were told to get on one truck and Paula and Ellen and the other women were told to get on another truck. After they left the village, the truck with the men stopped. The men were told to get off the truck and that they were free to leave. As the men started to walk away they were all shot. The truck with the women continued on to Périgueux, than to the French internment camp in Drancy and from there they were deported to Auschwitz-Birkenau extermination camp where they had ID numbers tattooed on their arms. Fortunately, Paula and Ellen survived, and I have personally seen those ugly numbers.

The incredible part of this story is that after my father and I arrived in the United States in 1950, my father, who was then widowed, met and married in 1951 in New York a German lady who was also widowed, Paula Baer, who became my step-mother. It turned out that her deceased husband was the brother of Willy Baer who was murdered in Saint Pancrace. Over the years we have remained in touch with the surviving French Baer family.

A heart breaking story that must be mentioned concerns my second cousin Florette Feissel, some fifteen years my senior. She also lived in Mulhouse and, together with her parents and brother, was a refugee traveling, like us, from Mulhouse to Lyon, then Chaudanne-Castellane, but ending up in the small city of Périgueux, the main town in the Dordogne. There Florette worked at L'Aide Sociale Israélite, an organization which played a major role in helping Jewish refugees in the area. On April 4, 1944, German soldiers arrived at the office of L'Aide Sociale Israélite where

Florette was working and arrested the five Jewish persons working there, including Florette Feissel. On April 13,1944, they were put on a train with many others bound for the extermination camp at Auschwitz-Birkenau.

I am setting out the following tragic and heroic story concerning Florette Feissel. In the cattle car bound for Auschwitz-Birkenau there was a little girl who was alone and, of course, frightened. My cousin took her under her wing. When they arrived in Auschwitz, the standard practice was for incoming deportees to walk past a German officer who would tell each able person to walk to the right which led to the labor camp. Older and infirm persons and children, were told to walk to the left which led to the gas chamber. My cousin walked past the German officer holding the little girl's hand. He told my cousin to let go of the little girl's hand and to walk to the right. When she refused to let go of the little girl's hand, both were told to walk to the left, which meant the gas chamber. Florette Feissel was murdered on April 16, 1944.

Florette's brother, Léon Feissel, who along with their parents were also refugees in Périgueux, was active in the French underground. After the war they returned to Mulhouse, and some years later Léon Feissel committed suicide, never able to overcome the trauma of what had happened to his sister and of his own war experience. I have been told this by Léon's daughter, Catherine Feissel, with whom I have been in touch. My parents were close to Florette and Léon Feissel's parents. They were the last persons we visited before my father and I emigrated to the United States.

After the war we moved back to Mulhouse in June, 1945. Our stay in Mulhouse from June 1945 to July 1950, from age 8 to 13, represents the final stage of my early life (annex 5 and 8).

When we returned to Mulhouse, we rented an apartment at 44 rue Hubner. In this four-story walk-up, our apartment was on the third floor. It was a two-bedroom apartment with a kitchen and a living room. There was no central heating. We had a coal stove in the kitchen for cooking, for heating water, and for heating the kitchen. It is there that we spent most of the day and ate our meals. We had a radio, but no telephone. We also had a coal stove in the living room which we seldom used. Our bathroom (no bathtub) was outside the apartment half a flight up from our apartment. Since we had no bathtub, we would go to the municipal bath once a week to take a bath.

The bedrooms were unheated. My parents would put a hot water bottle in my bed to warm it. I wore "bed shoes" (thick woolen socks) to make going to bed more comfortable. Every evening, my parents placed a piece of chocolate on my pillow which they called a "bett hupfer" (a bed jumper) which I would eat as I went to bed. It tasted very good, but was not good for my teeth. I also recall hopping into bed with my mother on some mornings. Even though life was more normal, I was still haunted by bad dreams. After returning to Mulhouse I would frequently wake up during the night with nightmares which continued after coming to the United States. No doubt a consequence of the war years.

The conditions in Mulhouse after our return were still bad. The city was seriously damaged during the final year of the war. Provisions in stores, including groceries, for several years after the war, were very limited. We were fortunate to receive Care packages on a regular basis from the two sisters of my mother (the Einsteins) who had emigrated to the United States in 1938. They sent us every day food and house items which were not available in France after the war. The items received were, of course, identified in English which we could not read. We often did not know how to use them. I recall one item in particular: corn flakes. We had never seen corn flakes and could not figure out how to eat them. We did not know that milk should be added, so we ate the cereal dry. We were not impressed.

The first job I remember my father had in Mulhouse was as a window decorator in the local department store. My father was very proud of his ability to print, including addresses on envelops as well as signs in store windows. I remember the store where he worked had an escalator up to the second floor. It was the hit of the town. He later became a manager in a factory that manufactured wool. As a wounded veteran, he received a modest pension which did not go very far in post-war pricing.

I had few toys. The one toy I remember receiving was an inexpensive wooden scooter with wooden wheels. Despite it's being very modest, I was quite pleased and enjoyed riding it. On Saturday evenings we sometimes went to a café for coffee or a soft drink and pastries and to listen to live music.

My mother was a very orthodox western European Jew. My father was more secular but adhered to her practices out of respect for her beliefs. She followed orthodox practices, such as making beef meat kosher when there was no kosher butcher. We had a strictly kosher home even during World War Two when we lived under constant fear of German arrest and deportation. A kosher home means that dairy products and meat products cannot be eaten together, nor can they be eaten on the same dishes. One had to wait three hours after eating a dairy or meat product before eating the other type of product. Every year prior to Passover, my mother would thoroughly clean the kitchen and its cupboards to ensure it was ready for Passover. I don't remember how my mother handled the situation during the war.

The main meal of the week was always Friday evening dinner to celebrate the beginning of the Sabbath, a happy and comforting occasion in the worst of times. Every Friday evening dinner, my father would put his hand on my head, say a prayer, and bless me. When we were back in Mulhouse, we always had carp for Friday dinner. On Saturday evenings we celebrated the end of Sabbath. I still have the elaborate silver Havdallah spice box and the silver wine goblet which, together with a braided candle, were used to celebrate the end of Sabbath (annex 1). In Mulhouse, on highholiday dinners, we had chicken which at that time was the most expensive meat available (more expensive than beef). There were numerous occasions, including during the war, when for religious reasons my mother would fast, including on the anniversary of the death of her father and her mother.

Every Saturday morning and, of course, on the holidays, we went to the synagogue in Mulhouse. The synagogue was an imposing structure built in 1849 in neoclassical style. It was damaged by the Germans during their occupation in World War Two, but the structure was saved when it was used as an annex to the local theater company. It was restored soon after the war. The synagogue in Mulhouse was a western European orthodox synagogue. Men sat in the main hall and the women sat in the upstairs balcony.

After the war in Mulhouse we only associated with Jewish families. I only had Jewish friends. I belonged to the Boys Scouts. At that time in Alsace, Boy Scout troops were segregated by religion. On one occasion my parents sent me to a Jewish summer camp. My best friend was Michel Kuflik who lived nearby and whose parents owned a clothing store. The Kufliks were a family of some means and as a result, as the war approached in 1939, they were able to escape the war by moving to Switzerland which only allowed persons with significant financial means to immigrate. They returned to Mulhouse after the war.

Some of the most exciting events after our return to Mulhouse were the visits of my cousins Ernest

Fleischman and Sam Weimersheimer who came to see us while on furlough from the United States Army. They brought us gifts, including chewing gum and ball point pens, which we had never seen before. They were quite a hit. I was so proud when they walked with us in town in their army uniforms.

Soon after our return to Mulhouse, my mother became ill. Her illness gradually worsened. Since medication was often not available in France soon after the war, we frequently travelled to Basel, Switzerland, some twenty miles southeast of Mulhouse to buy medication. As her illness grew worse, she had to be hospitalized for extended periods. On one occasion, when I was 11 or 12 years old, I was sent to a Jewish orphanage for boys in Haguenau, a town some 85 miles north of Mulhouse. I was there for about a month. I remember almost nothing about the orphanage. What I do recall is that on some occasions a few of the boys and I would hide behind the bushes and smoke a cigarette and then eat toothpaste thinking it would hide the smell.

As I mentioned earlier, my father had suffered from rheumatic fever as a child which, coupled with his being wounded in battle in 1940, seriously impaired him for the rest of his life. As we know, rheumatic fever can now be easily treated and treatment for heart problems was almost non-existent. Medication for treating heart problems was very limited, mainly digitalis, and surgical procedures were impossible. He was frequently hospitalized in Clairvivre and in Mulhouse and unable to live a normal life.

With both my parents being frequently ill, I was always worried about their dying. For example, when my parents went shopping in Mulhouse and did not return at the time expected, I would worry that something had happened to them. Similarly, when I was in summer camp or at the orphanage and I had not received a letter on the day expected, I became worried. This worry stayed with me throughout my early life and lingered after I came to in the United States. Anxiety doesn't remain in the place it began, but follows you wherever you go. Over the years, I have learned to repress my feelings.

On November 22, 1949, in the early morning there was a knock at our apartment door. My father answered. When he came back he told me "we do not have a mother anymore". My mother was 44 when she died. Had my mother lived, my life would have evolved very differently. She was buried in the Jewish cemetery of Mulhouse. I am sure we sat shiva, but I can't remember. I have beautiful portraits of my mother and of my father taken in Altenstadt ca 1938 and in Mulhouse ca 1948 (annex 5).

Following her death, my father was very good at keeping us busy. I remember in particular, we would often attend the local soccer team matches and sometimes would accompany the team to watch them play on the road. A few days before we left Mulhouse for the United States, we went to watch the Harlem Globetrotters play in town.

My mother's sisters' families, Gertrud and Frida Einstein, sponsored our immigration to the United States. However, because of my mother's illness, we had to delay our departure. Following my mother's death, my father made arrangements for us to emigrate to the United States. Since our only relatives who were still alive after World War Two were those who lived in the United States, we decided to postpone my bar mitzvah until after we arrived in New York.

We departed from Cherbourg on the Queen Mary on July 20, 1950, and arrived in New York on July 25, 1950 (annex 9). I don't remember much about the trip, except the language problem. Since the Queen Mary was a British ship most of the help on board, including the waiters, were British with limited ability to speak anything but English.

I had spoken French with my friends and at school, however throughout our years together, my parents and I always spoke German at home. Neither my father nor I knew a word of English when we left France. Being on a British ship, it was our first exposure to the challenge and necessity of learning a new language rapidly. It would be especially difficult for my father. After my father died in 1968, there was no one to speak German with, and I had no desire to remember it.

A second immediate necessity was to understand the value of different currencies.

Sometimes when we bought items on board we would receive change in American money. Figuring out its value was a problem. I remember one instance, when the change I received was a dime. Since dime sounded like demi, which in French means half, I assumed a dime was half a dollar.

My first sight of the life in the United States was when the Queen Mary was docking in New York on the afternoon of July 25, 1950. It was a warm July day. I was struck that all the cars on the pier were yellow. I thought it was very strange that all the cars had the same yellow color. Of course, I found out later that they were cabs. As we got off the ship, my aunts and uncles and their two sons Herbert and David, met us at the pier. My cousin David gave me a coke. My exposure to the United States had begun.

* * * * *

ANNEX 1

Silver wine goblet and havdallah spice box used to celebrate the end of the Sabbath.

My grandfather's shooting trophies.

ANNEX 2

Jews' Street in Altenstadt before the war. The synagogue is the large building on the right. The house of my parents and grandmother is a few buildings up on the same side of the street.

Altenstadt Synagogue built in 1802 with community center in back.

Interior of Altenstadt Synagogue.

ANNEX 3

Me at age 14 months, held by one of my cousins.
Three and a half years later my cousin will be murdered in an extermination camp.

ANNEX 4

My mother's French passport upon leaving Germany on March 27, 1939.

At the bottom of the left page is my name as her 21-month-old dependent.

ANNEX 5

My mother and father ca 1938

My mother and father ca 1948.

My mother and father behind our house in Clairvivre.

My father with his French Army unit in 1940. He is in the front row, the first on the right.

ANNEX 6

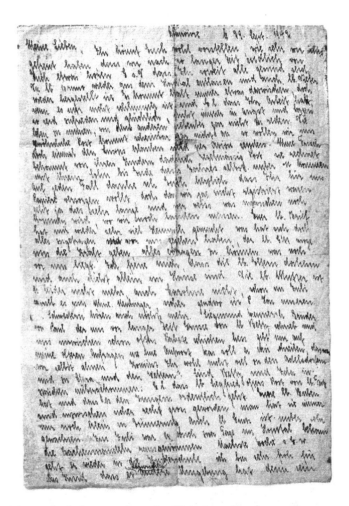

My mother's letter written in Clairvivre, Dordogne, France on
September 29, 1942 and mailed to her two sisters in New York.

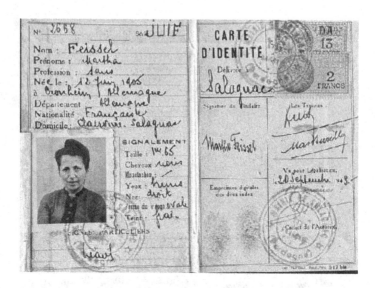

The identity cards of my mother and father while in Clairvivre with the word JUIF (JEW) highlighted.

Alsaciens Lorrains juifs dans les Basses-Alpes à la fin de 1940

Noms	Année de naissance
Feissel Marthe	1905 «
Feissel Gustave	1937 «

List of Jews from Alsace Lorraine living in the Basses Alpes at the end of 1940.

The list contains the names 109 Jews of which my mother and I are two.

My refugee card which states
that I am a refugee because I was expelled from Alsace.

ANNEX 8

Mulhouse 1948, age 11

Age 5, Clairvivre.

Outside my father's hospital room, ca 1943-44, age 7, Clairvivre.

MA CLASSE A L'ECOLE DE CLAIRVIVRE

My class in Clairvivre ca 1943. I am the second to the left of the teacher.

My father and I on the Queen Mary, July 1950.

Printed in the United States
by Baker & Taylor Publisher Services